Santa Carving

with Myron Bowman

To Myron Bowman,
a Master Woodcarver
and my Friend!

Don Dewey 95©

FOX BOOKS

Fox Chapel Publishing Co Inc.

Box 7948
Lancaster, PA 17604

© 1996 by Fox Chapel Publishing Company Inc.

Publisher: Alan Giagnocavo
Project Editor: Ayleen Stellhorn
Desktop Specialist: Robert Altland, Altland Design
Cover Photography: Bob Polett, VMI Communications

ISBN # 1–56523–076–0

To order your copy of this book,
please send check or money order
for $12.95 plus $2.50 shipping to:
Fox Chapel Book Orders
Box 7948
Lancaster, PA 17604–7948

Try your favorite book supplier first!

Table of Contents

About the Author

How many of you have been to Branson, Silver Dollar City, or a woodcarving show, and been totally amazed with the carvers and their work? I was first introduced to carving by Pete Engler at Engler's Block in Branson, Missouri. Pete was willing to share his joy of carving with me. I will always thank him for that and try to pass that joy on to the people I meet. After I got my first set of tools, which I still use, I was hooked on carving. That was many years ago and much has changed since then. What began as a hobby has turned into a full time career.

When I first began carving. I carved faces and flowers on walking sticks. I worked on perfecting that for about a year then I worked with chip carving for a year. I then became interested in carving Santas. I soon realized there was a great demand for Santas in any style or size. Each year I carve several new designs, which helps to keep things interesting for me and my customers. It's fun to hear and see the reactions my carvings have on people. I've been at a show carving at my booth and all of the sudden hear someone just bust out laughing. I look up to see the person holding one of my Santas or walking sticks laughing at the expression on the face. It makes me happy to bring a smile to others through my art.

I started by selling my carvings at local craft shows, then branched out to shows and woodcarving competitions in surrounding states. I currently sell my carvings through Mountain Woodcarvers in Estes Park, Colorado, and the Bob Lewis Art Gallery in Winfield, Kansas. In November, 1993, I was approached by Hallmark, Inc. They commissioned me to carve a set of four Santas for Christmas 1994. That series is called the Woodland Santa. For Christmas 1995 I carved a cowboy Santa that was sold in Hallmark stores across the country. I am also working with Crescent Enterprises on making reproductions of my work to be sold worldwide. I have taught classes both in my own studio at my home in Winfield, Kansas, and also in several locations in Colorado. I have taught at the Wood Carvers Rendezvous in Creede, the Como Experience in Como, The Wildwood Studio in Louisville as well as the Mountain Woodcarvers in Estes Park. On October 1, 1990, I quit a full-time job to keep up with the demand of carving. My only regret is that I was not able to pursue carving as a career sooner.

Several years ago, Pam Johnson of Mountain Woodcarvers suggested I do a book on how to carve a Santa. She kept pushing me and finally got me together with Fox Chapel Publishing, and here I am. I would like to thank Pam, her husband Sky and her father Maurice Walk for all of their help. From the first time I walked into their store with a little Santa standing on a chimney to setting up classes in their woodcarving school they have always been supportive of me. They have become good friends.

I live outside Winfield, Kansas, with my wife Brenda, our two daughters Sara and Beth, two dogs and seven cats. My shop is next door to the house so I don't have much trouble with traffic, except for the cats.

I remember when I first began carving I just wanted to be able to carve a face. Now I am teaching others how to carve faces. My biggest reward is to have a student come up to me at the end of a seminar and tell me they learned something. I hope you will also learn something from this, my first book.—Myron Bowman

Special Thanks

My ability to complete this book was made possible by many good friends. The drawing of me on the title page of this book was done by a very good friend of mine, Don Dane of Olathe, Kansas. The photographs were taken by a local artist Gary Hana, of Winfield, Kansas. My ability to continue the work I enjoy would not be possible if it weren't for the generous people I have met along the way. I would like to thank the following: Bill and Betty Craig, Don and Debby Dane, George and Judi Barnard, Gene and Donela Roberts, Jack and Reggie Daviau, Jon and Donna Nelson, Mr. and Mrs. Pat Patterson, Herb and Ann Schrader, Bill and Geri Gartner, Jack and Vicki Portice, Fred Williamson and "Blackie" Blackburn. These friends have opened their homes and kitchens to me and my family. The support shown to me by these and the many other woodcarvers I have met has made it possible for me to do what I truly enjoy.

Photo Gallery

Carving Step-by-Step

The Santa I've chosen to carve in this demonstration is called Bronco Bill Claus. Beginning carvers will learn many basic carving techniques by following along step-by-step. More advanced carvers who are familiar with the basics of carving, but not with the basics of carving Santas, will find countless helpful tips and techniques throughout the demonstration.

Wood Choice

This Santa has been carved from a block of Northern basswood. I find basswood an easy wood to carve and perfect for beginning carvers. It is available at carving supply stores and most lumber yards. Other easy-to-carve woods include catalpa, aspen, bristlecone pine, butternut and white walnut.

When choosing wood, use the following guidelines to pick the best piece for your carving.

For this Santa, you'll need a block of wood 4" wide x 4" deep x 7" high.

Tools

You'll need the following basic woodcarving tools to carve this Santa:

Calipers
#9 3mm u-gouge
#7 fish tail gouge
1/8" veiner
1" chisel
60-degree v-tool
1/16" veiner
bench knife
1/4" v-tool
1/4" u-gouge

Applying the Pattern

The pattern for this Santa can be found on page XX. There are several methods for transferring the pattern to your block of wood. The method I prefer uses carbon paper. Simply photocopy the pattern, enlarging or reducing it if necessary to fit your block. Then place a piece of carbon paper, carbon-side down, behind the wood, and the pattern. Finally, trace over the pattern lines with a sharp

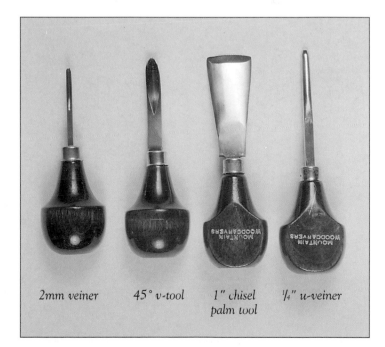

2mm veiner   45° v-tool   1" chisel palm tool   1/4" u-veiner

object, such as a pencil. When you remove the pattern and the carbon paper, the lines of the pattern will appear on the wood.

A Word About Safety

I do all my carving with a vise holding the block of wood. This allows you to exert better control over your tools because you can use both hands to cut; the vise holds the wood. I suggest using a carving screw and carving arm to get easier access to all areas.

It is also very important that you keep all knives, gouges and chisels very sharp. Sharp tools will cut through the wood easier, preventing a slip of the tool due to forcing a dull-edged blade through wood. Sharpening can be done a number of ways, and each carver seems to have a method he prefers over all the others. I suggest purchasing a book that covers sharpening methods in depth or taking a class in which the instructor takes some time to explain his preferred sharpening techniques.

If you are unfamiliar the tools used in this demonstration, practice making basic cuts on a block of scrap wood. Make upward sweeping strokes with the v-tools, downward strokes with the u-gouges, broad strokes to remove wood with the fishtail gouges, and small detail cuts with the carving knife. Being familiar with your tools will help you control them and, lead to safer carving practices.

Some Important Terms

The following terms are used in the book. These are basic cuts used frequently in carving.

Stop Cut: Done with a carving knife. I use this cut to get a nice clean edge between two depths of wood. It is done by cutting with the tip of the knife to the point in the pattern where wood is to be removed. Excess wood is removed by cutting to the stop cut, usually at a 90 or 45 degree angle. The piece of wood you want to remove should easily come off after this cut. If not repeat both cuts until the piece falls out.

Saw Cut: This is another type of stop cut, a safer and more precise method used for the smaller details of carving. This cut is also done with a carving knife. Stab the tip of the knife into the wood fairly deep and move along the line in a sawing motion.

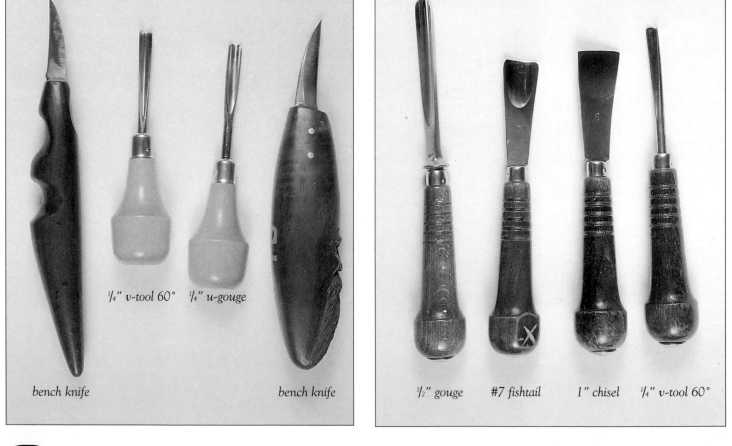

¼" v-tool 60°   ¼" u-gouge

bench knife   bench knife

½" gouge   #7 fishtail   1" chisel   ¼" v-tool 60°

Shaping the Santa's Body

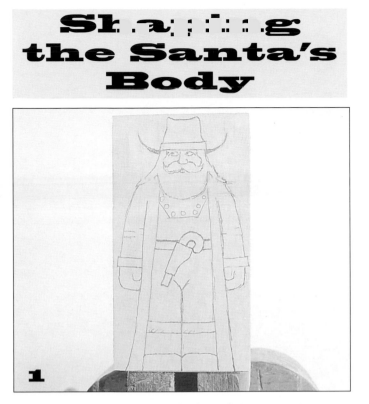

1

Begin with a 4" x 4" x 7" block of wood. I am using basswood. Transfer the pattern on to the front and side of the wood. This is easily done by placing a piece of carbon paper between the wood and the pattern and tracing over the pattern lines with a pencil or other pointed object.

2

As you can see in this illustration, the bottom lines of the hat are angled. This allows the hat to be tilted back slightly on the head. The bottom of the brim on the back is about 1/4" lower than the front.

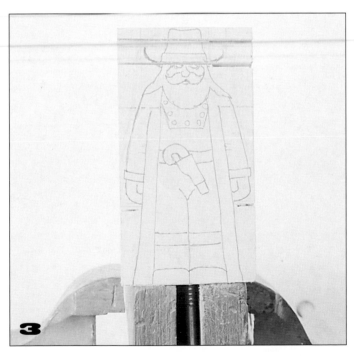

3

With a hand saw, make cuts as shown, sawing in from the side first. There will be three cuts made from each side: one above the brim of the hat, one below the brim of the hat at the angle, and one below the mittens. Remember, these cuts will be angled. Stop sawing 1/8" away form the pattern lines. You will also cut from the front and the back, above and below the hat brim.

4

With a #5 fishtail chisel remove wood as shown. Always leave 1/8" excess wood outside the pattern marks.

Still using the #5 fishtail chisel, remove the wood below the brim of the hat as shown.

Turn the piece to the side. Draw in the side view of the Santa as shown. A pattern is not necessary for these lines. Simply follow the photo and approximate the pencil marks as closely as possible.

Continue to use the #5 fishtail chisel to remove the wood below brim of hat on the front and the back of the Santa.

Work all around the hat, moving back and forth from front to back to remove the wood. Again, remember to keep 1/8" away from the pencil lines.

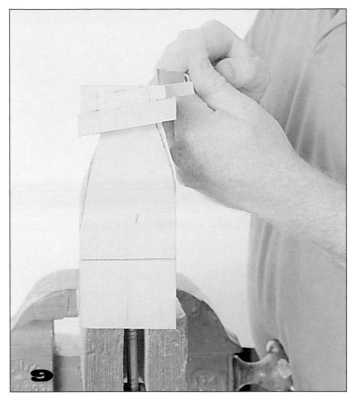

Still using the #5 fishtail chisel, remove the wood above the brim of hat to the lines drawn on side of piece.

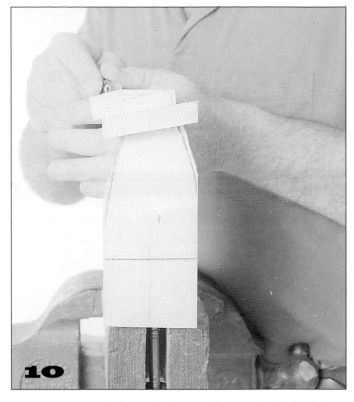

Remove the wood above the brim of hat on the back of the hat as well.

Viewed from the top, the Santa's hat should now look like this. Wood has been removed from all sides of the hat brim.

Use a 1" chisel to begin to round the brim of the hat.

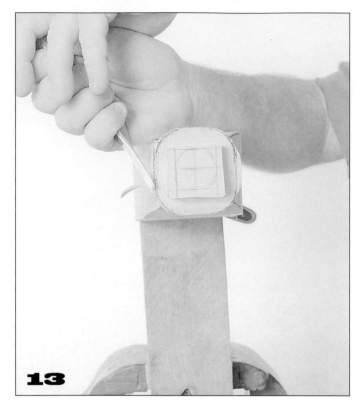

Continue rounding the brim of the hat with a 1" chisel. Remove excess wood to pattern lines drawn in earlier.

Once the brim of the hat has been shaped, use a 1/2" u-gouge to round the riser of the hat.

Draw in a pencil line on the hat to indicate the angle of the top of the riser and cut to this line.

Viewed from the side, the Santa should now look like this.

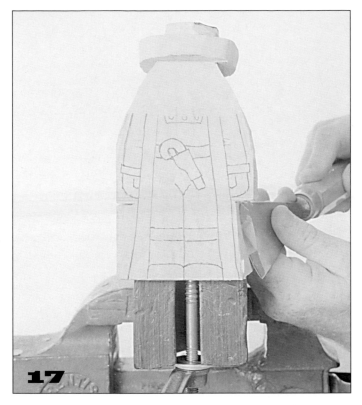

17

Remove wood below the mittens from each side using a #5 fishtail chisel. Remember to leave $1/8"$ excess outside the pattern lines. Do not cut off the pattern lines.

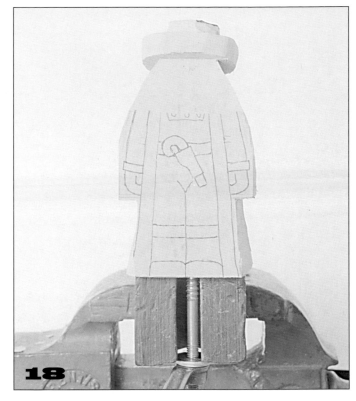

18

The Santa should now look like this from the front.

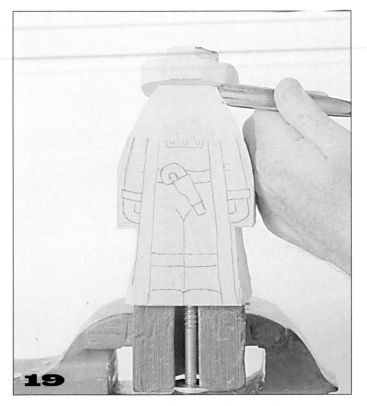

19

Now, use a $1/2"$ u-gouge to remove the wood on the corners below the hat, rounding the body of your piece.

20

Viewed from the front, the Santa should look like this.

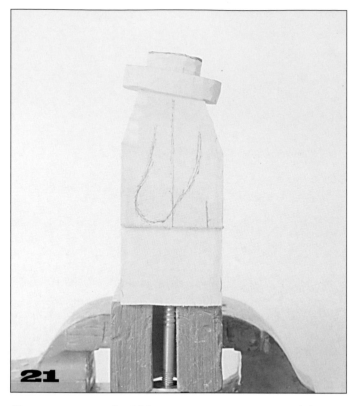

Continue using the 1/2" u-gouge to remove wood from the front and back corners below the hat.

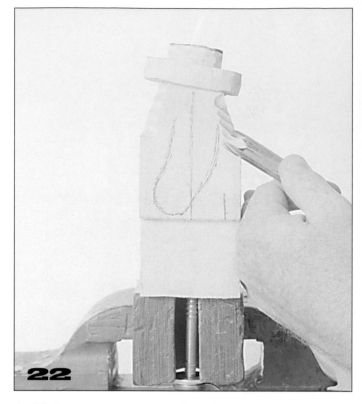

Hold the u-gouge at an angle and make upward sweeping strokes to remove the wood.

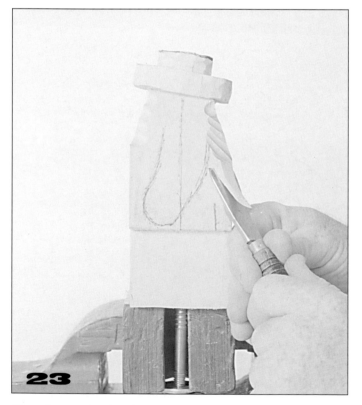

Switch to a 1" chisel, cutting in an upward direction as shown. Remove wood up to the bottom of the hat following the pattern lines.

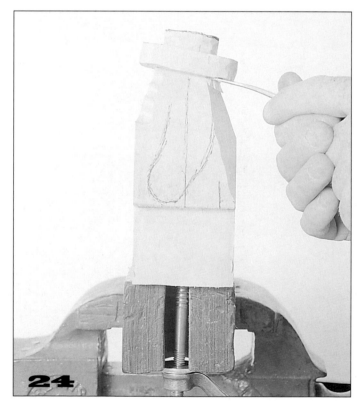

Using the same chisel, make a stop cut below the brim of the hat on the back of the piece.

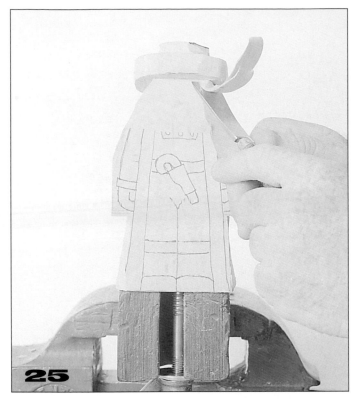

25

Still using the chisel, cut upward to remove the wood under the brim. Continue removing wood in this manner around the entire piece.

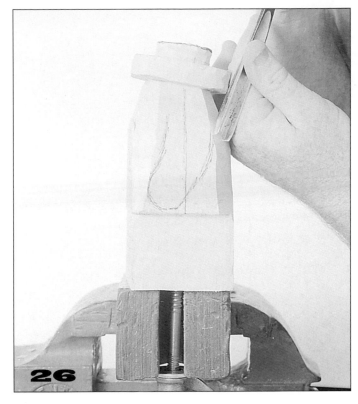

26

With a 1/2" u-gouge cut downward as shown, removing excess wood from the back of the piece to define the arm. It is important to cut in this direction to prevent the wood on the back of the arm from splintering.

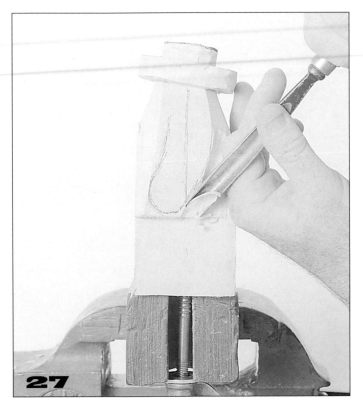

27

Using the 1/2" u-gouge, continue to make downward cuts to define the arms and mittens.

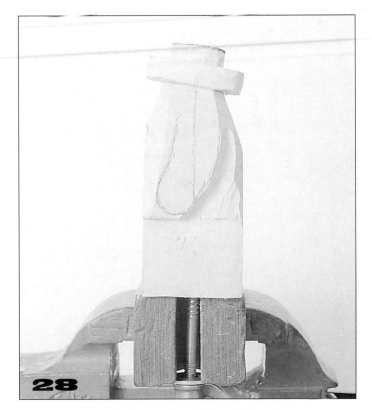

28

At this point, the Santa should look like this.

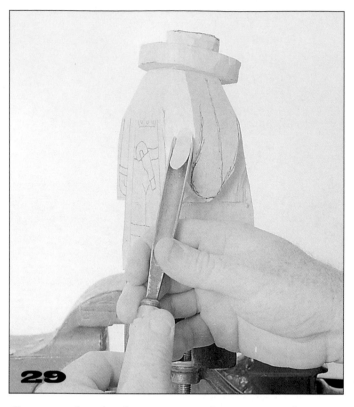

29

Cut upward with a large u-gouge, bringing out the arms on both sides of the body.

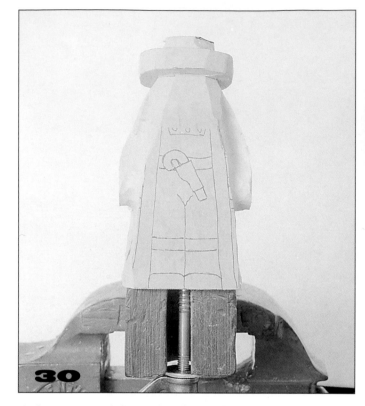

30

A front view of the Santa shows the shaped hat and arms.

ADDING WRINKLES

Adding wrinkles or creases to Santa's clothing is one of those extra touches that will make your finished piece more appealing. Well-placed wrinkles will also add to the appearance of a jolly Santa who's just a little too big for his own britches, so to speak.

Wrinkles and creases can be added to Santa's pants, overcoat and shirt. The most obvious places for wrinkles are at the elbows, knees and across the back. You won't actually be carving the wrinkles until after the body has been shaped, but it's best to plan for wrinkles now so that you have enough wood in these areas once your Santa has been shaped.

Gouges are the best tools to carve wrinkles. Use a 1/2" gouge for larger wrinkles and a 1/4" gouge for smaller wrinkles. Simply remove a small sliver of wood with a slow, controlled sweep of the gouge. Keep the wrinkles short in length, and don't go overboard. Too many wrinkles will detract from your finished piece.

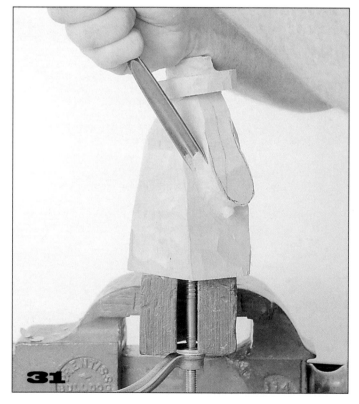

31

Next, define the arms with a large v-tool. Work both the front and the back of arms on both sides.

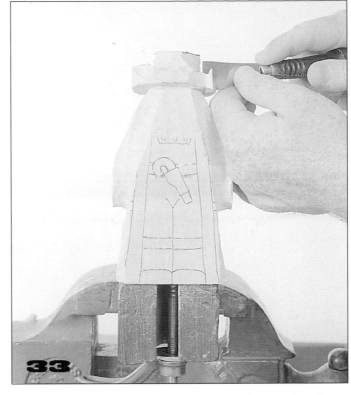

Using a 1/4" u-gouge begin hollowing out the brim of the hat. Shaping the hat is an involved procedure that will be completed over several steps. At this time, just take off enough wood to show the scoop of the brim.

Carefully round the brim of the hat with a 1" chisel.

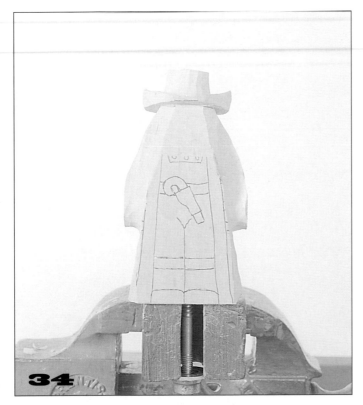

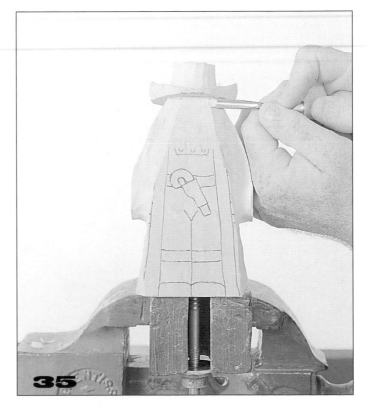

The hat should now look like this. The brim has been hollowed out so that both sides of the hat appear to curl inward toward the crown.

Using a 1/4" u-gouge, begin to define the head on both sides as shown.

Leave plenty of excess wood on the front of the Santa to create a face later.

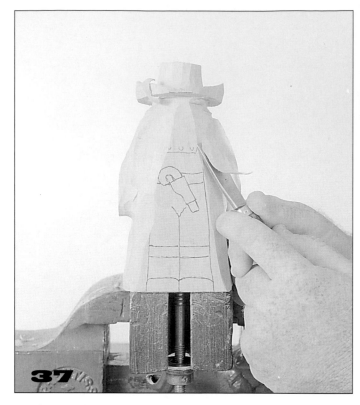

With a 1" chisel round the corners in front of the arms. These cuts will begin rounding the body.

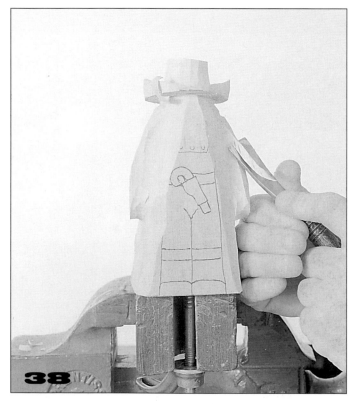

Continue using the 1" chisel to round the corners on arms.

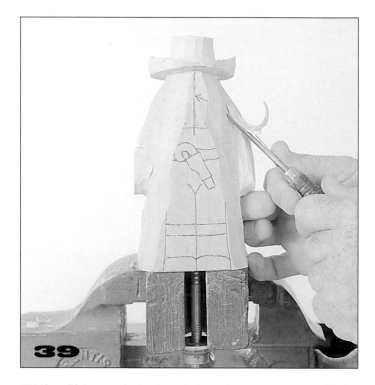

With a 1/4" v-tool, further define the arms next to body. Then, draw a centerline vertically from brim of hat downward as shown. Round the corners up to this line with 1" chisel. Cut upward, stopping at the centerline and leaving a wedge.

Continue to use the v-tool to define the arms next to the body on both the front and the back of the Santa.

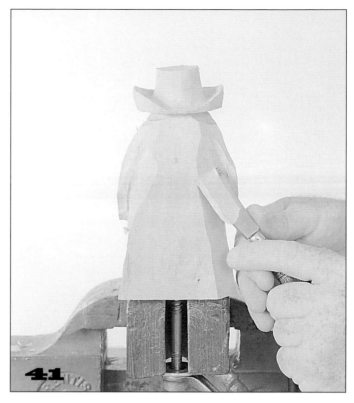

With a 1" chisel, round the corners on the back of the body.

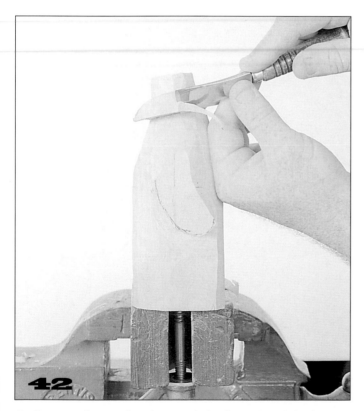

Still using the 1" chisel, round the bottom of the hat brim as shown, carefully removing the excess wood to the point where the hat meets the head.

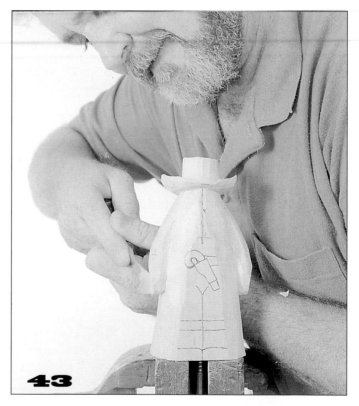

Moving down to the mittens, use a 1" chisel to cut an angle on the mittens as shown.

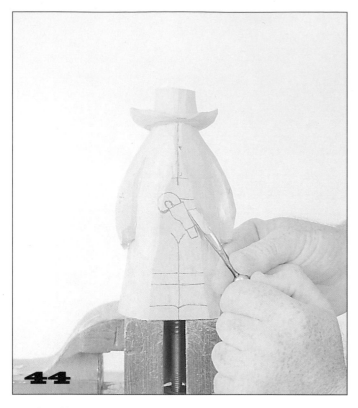

44

With a ¹/4" u-gouge bring out the holster by removing wood around the holster and the candy cane. Above the holster, make cuts with an upward sweep of the tool.

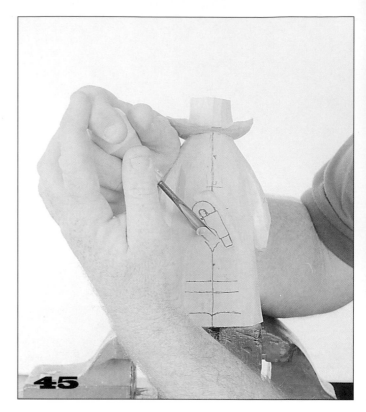

45

Below the holster, remove wood in downward strokes. Remove enough wood to make the holster stick out about ¹/4" from the body.

WHAT MAKES A SANTA "WESTERN STYLE?"

Picture a cowboy in your mind. Those elements that make him a stereotypical cowboy—the hat, the gun and holster, the lasso, the boots and spurs—are the same elements that you'll want to add to your western-style Santa.

For the Santa in this demonstration, I've added a large cowboy hat and a holster stuffed not with a gun, but with a red and white striped candy cane. I cover techniques for carving both of these items in the carving demonstration.

If you need help carving additional items, check other books on carving cowboy figures. Fox Books publishes several titles. You might also try searching for reference material at your local library on cowboys and the Old West.

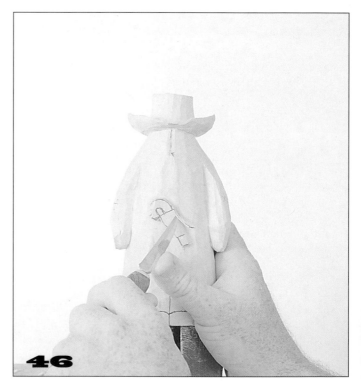

46

Using a carving knife carefully begin rounding the candy cane and the holster, cutting away any excess wood. Note that I am using upward cuts, following in the direction of the grain on the holster.

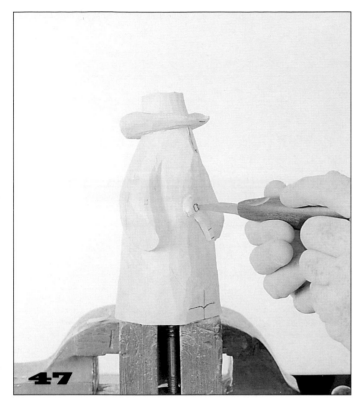

Still using the carving knife, make stop cuts where the candy cane meets the body. Use the knife in a sawing motion to trace the crook of the candy cane.

Cut behind the candy cane allowing the center piece to come out. If the center piece does not come out, repeat stop cuts until it does. Note: I recommend a carving knife with a thin blade for this particular step. If you do not have one, an X-acto™ knife will work well.

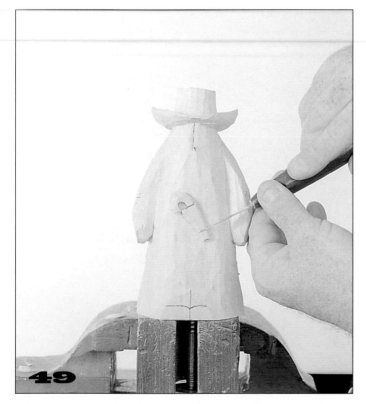

Use the carving knife to round the candy cane, defining both the holster and the candy cane.

When the candy cane and holster have been rounded to your liking, move to the back of the Santa. Use a 1" chisel to round the back of the Santa's body more.

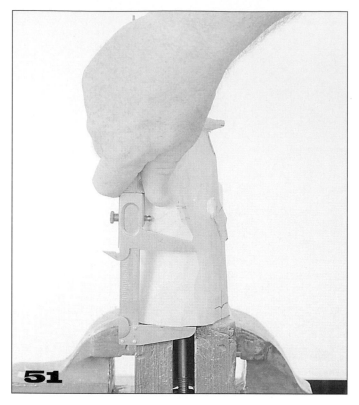

Use calipers to measure the distance from the bottom of the wood to the bottom of the mittens. This distance should be approximately 2¹/₂". Trim the mittens to make even.

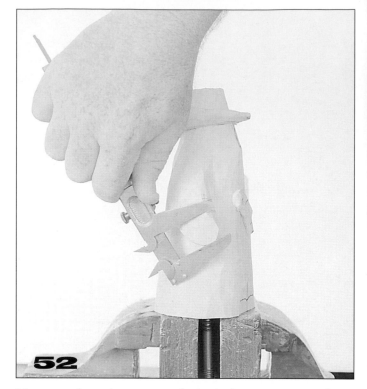

Now use the calipers to make sure the mittens are the same length from tip to cuff. The cuff should be approximately ³/₄" from the bottom of the cuff to the tip of the mitten and ³/₈" wide. Draw guidelines on the wood with a pencil.

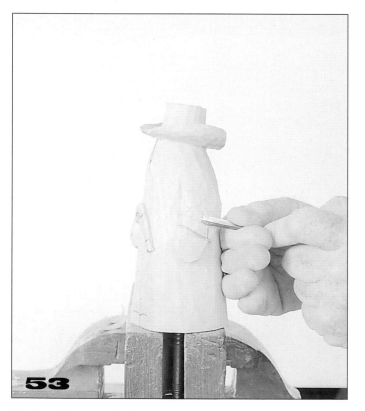

With a ¹/₄" v-tool define the cuff by making a 1/8" deep cut above the guidelines.

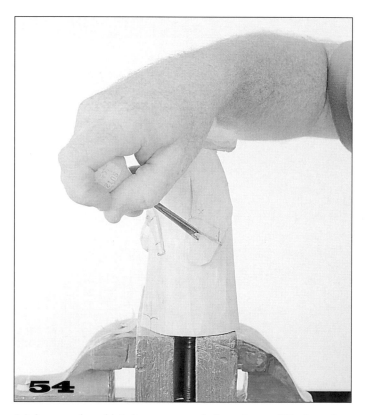

Make another ¹/₈" deep cut to define the cuff below the guidelines.

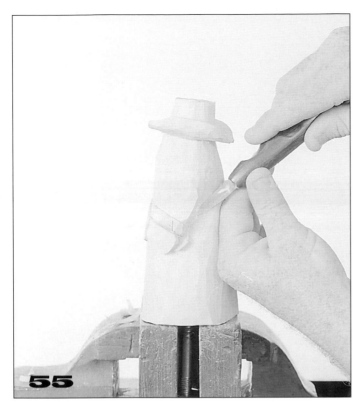

55

Using a carving knife, make a stop cut along the arm and the mitten on both the front and the back. To make the stop cut, lay the side of the knife against the body, then cut between the arm and the body.

56

Begin cleaning up excess wood above the cuff by cutting upward to create a smooth line for the arm and the mitten. Be sure to follow the grain and make cuts in direction shown.

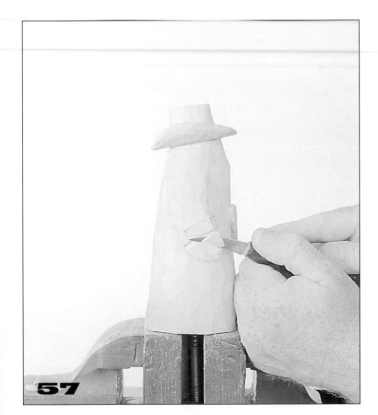

57

Clean up excess wood below the cuff by cutting downward. This will create a smooth line for the mitten. Again, be sure to follow the grain and cut in the direction shown.

Carving the Santa's Face

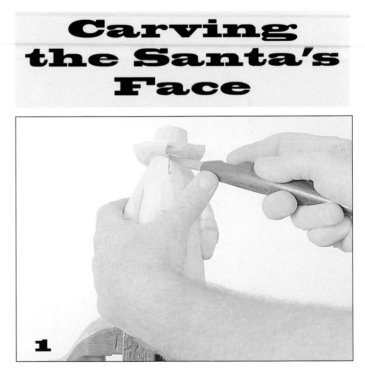

1

Now, let's carve a face. It's best to start on the face now because the facial features stick out farther than the coat. If the wedge on the face of your Santa is not very pronounced, make it so by removing wood up to the centerline, but not beyond.

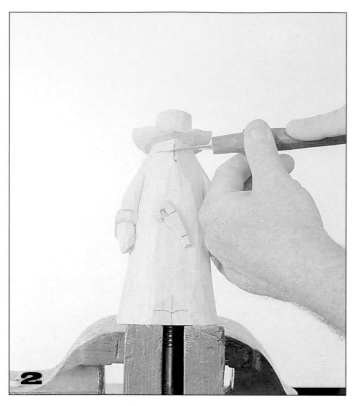

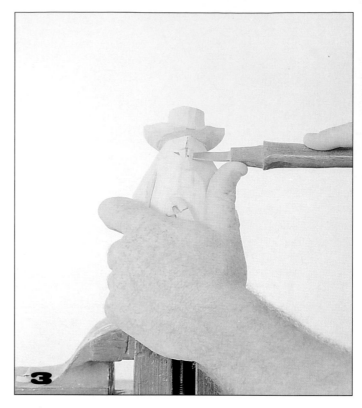

The first cut on a face is a stop cut to bring out the nose. This cut should be made ¹/₂" below the bottom of the brim of the hat. Make the cut ¹/₈" deep, straight into the wood with a carving knife.

With your carving knife, make a gradual, angling cut up from below to your stop cut at the bottom of the nose.

Viewed from the side, the Santa will look like this.

Draw a triangle from each edge of the previous cut to the base of the brim of the hat. This will form the nose.

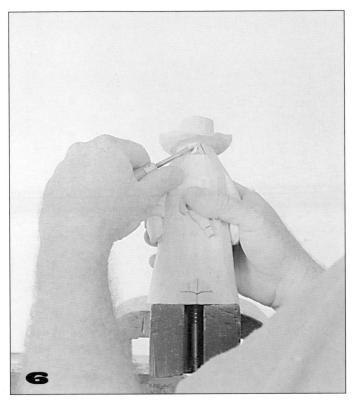

Using a 1/4" v-tool, cut along the sides of triangle from the base of the nose to the brim of hat. Be sure to leave the pencil line.

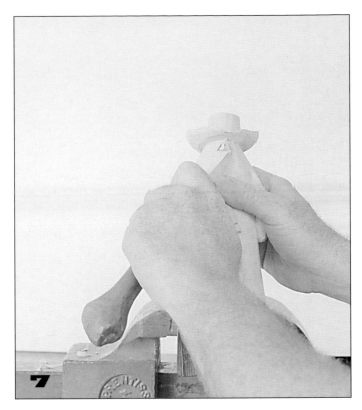

Next, draw a 45-degree angle cutting off the two lower corners of the triangle. Make a stop cut behind each corner.

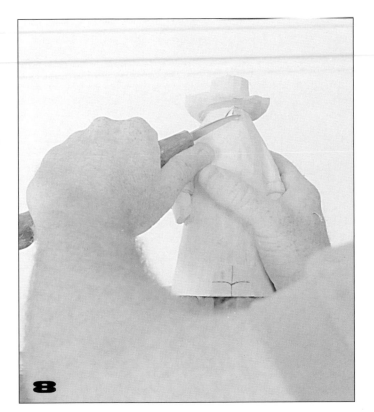

Make a 45-degree angle cut with the carving knife, rounding off the bottom of the nose.

With the carving knife held at the angle shown, cut off the very tip of the nose. Then, draw on the beard. Define the beard with a 1/4" v-tool. Remove any excess wood below the beard so that the beard sticks out 1/8" above the chest.

10

Now let's do some detail work on the face. Draw lines as shown to define the nostrils of the nose. With a v-tool, follow the line. Cut in an upward motion to round the upper edge of the nose.

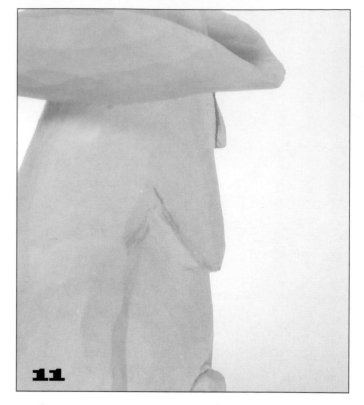

11

With a carving knife trim off any excess wood above the dotted line. This will form the forehead and bridge of the Santa's nose. The bridge of the nose should be 1/8" below the brim of the hat.

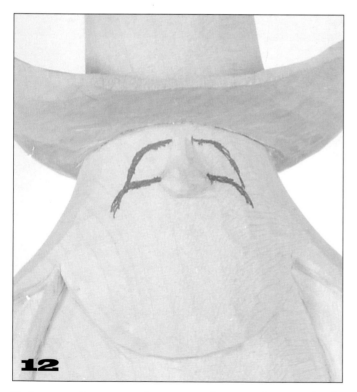

12

Before moving on to the eyes, make sure the nose looks similar to the nose of this Santa. Then, pencil in the area for the eyes as shown. The brow line should also be 1/8" below the brim of the hat.

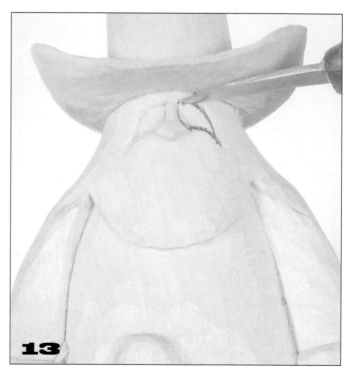

13

Using the carving knife make a saw cut around the eye area for both eyes. Starting at the center of each eye socket, cut to the saw cut. Leave the center of the eye area higher, creating a mound. Round the edges of the brow and cheek.

14

Using a 1/8" n-gouge, carefully cut in nostril holes as shown.

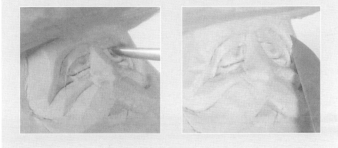

Placing the eyes on any carving is an important step that can make or break a carving. Placing the eyes on a western-style Santa can be especially tricky with those bushy eyebrows overshadowing them.

To avoid making mistakes that can't easily be fixed, mark in the eyes with a pencil first. Try to place the eyes evenly within the sockets—either to the left of both of the eyes or to the right of both of the eyes (or one to the left and one to the right if you *really* want a cross-eyed Santa). I recommend placing the pupils toward the top of the eye, just touching the upper lid. I don't recommend centering the pupils.

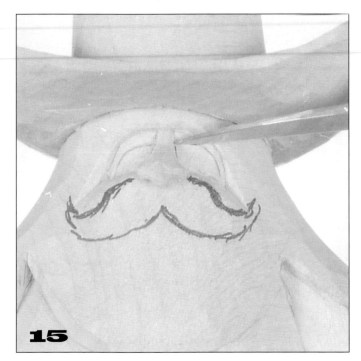

15

Make a saw cut with your carving knife to create the upper eyelid. Cut up from cheek to upper lid 1/32" depth. Pencil in a mustache as shown. The top of the mustache should start at the flare of the nostril, not below, or the mustache will be too low by the time it is trimmed.

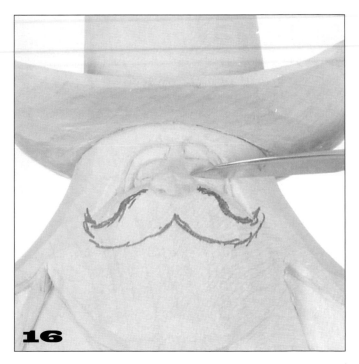

16

Next, define the lower eyelids by making a saw cut using the tip of the carving knife. Notice on the left of the picture how the outer edge of the lower eyelid flips up slightly. Starting 1/32" above the lower lid, cut at a downward angle toward the stop cut at the bottom of eyeball.

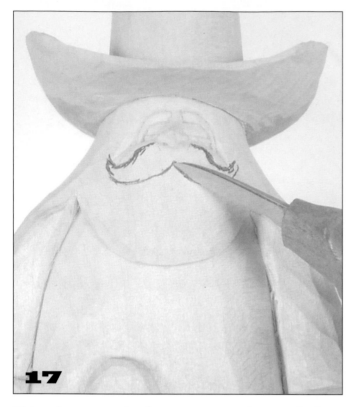

17

Using the carving knife, saw cut around mustache line. On the tip of the mustache, cut straight in. Do not angle down.

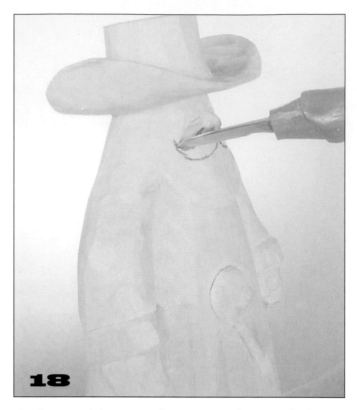

18

At the tip of the mustache, cut straight in with the carving knife. Do not angle down.

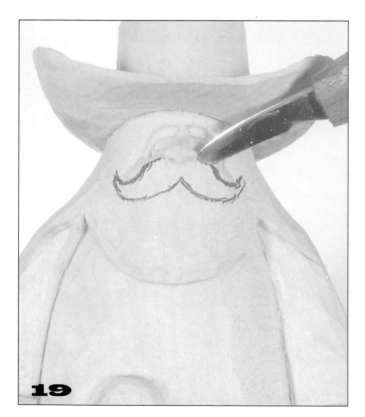

19

When saw cutting next to the nose, angle down slightly as shown.

20

Using your carving knife, cut to the stop cut, removing a thin layer of wood below the mustache. Round the mustache, top and bottom, cutting at an angle so the mustache appears rounded and full. On the top of the mustache, start cutting at the tip and cut toward the nose.

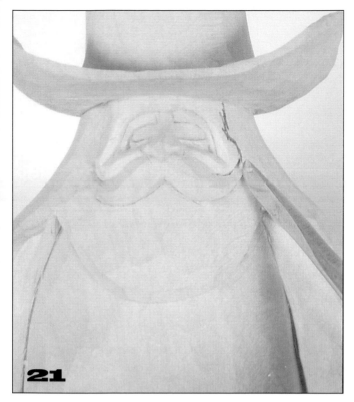

At this point, the mustache should look like this. Draw lines to mark the side of face area and the hair line. With a 1/4" v-tool start a cut at the outer tip of the mustache and follow the line upward to the brim of the hat.

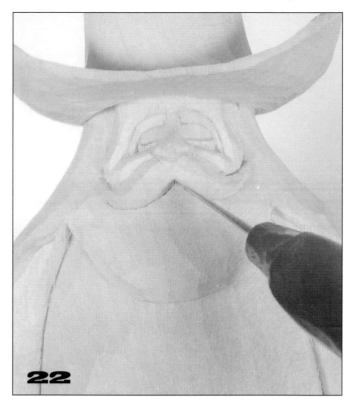

Using your carving knife make a stop cut along the contour of the mustache as shown. Cut a very small wedge of wood from under the mustache for the mouth, as shown with the dotted line.

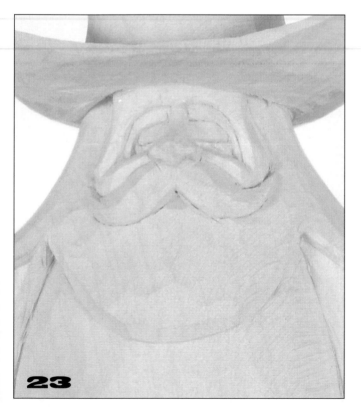

Make sure the face of the Santa is nice and round. The mouth opening should be noticeable. Pencil in lines as shown for the lower lip.

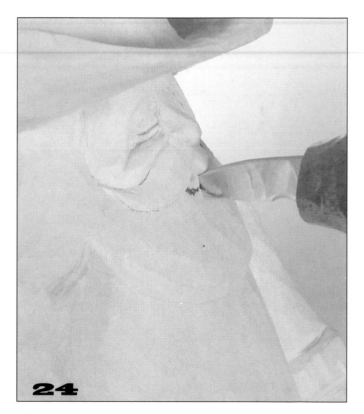

With the tip of carving knife cut an angle as shown to define the lower lip.

25

Continue defining the lower lip. Notice the temple area. The depth from the hair line to the front of the face is necessary to give the Santa a nice round face.

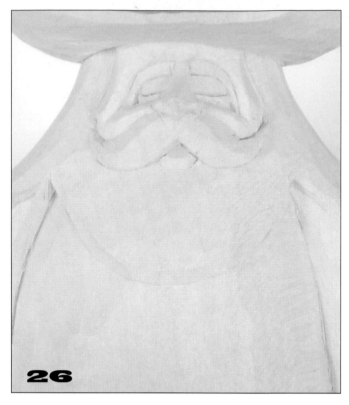

26

The Santa's face should now look like this.

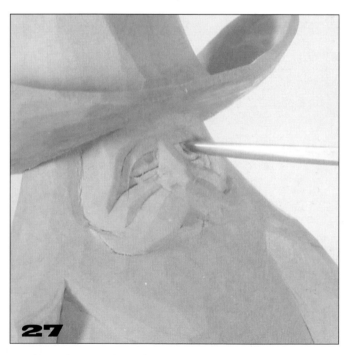

27

Draw in the pupils and make a stop cut between the upper eyelid and eyeball where the pupil is to be placed. Use a 1/8" u-gouge and an upward motion to scoop out the pupil. Be careful as you do not want to cut into the upper lid. If the pupil does not pop out, repeat the stop cut.

28

Add smile lines to the eyes. These can be easily made by using a carving knife to carve two notches just outside both eyes in the temple area.

28

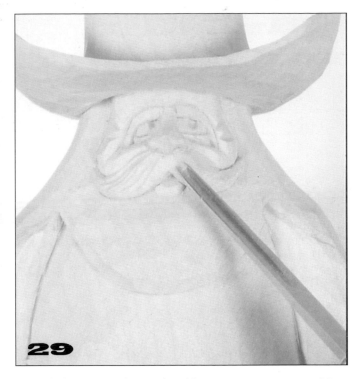

29

Detail the mustache with a $^{1}/_{16}$" or 2mm u-gouge. Use the tool in a flowing upward motion toward the nose. Then use the tool in a downward motion to detail the underside of the mustache. Use the same tools to detail the eyebrows. Use very small stokes angling outward around the brow line.

DETAILING SANTA'S BEARD

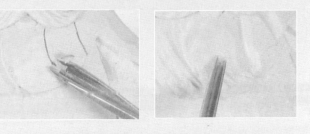

The most important thing to remember when detailing Santa's beard is to remove wood in flowing, curving sweeps—not straight lines. Removing wood in straight lines will give Santa's beard a stiff, unrealistic look. Flowing lines, on the other hand, will make the hair of Santa's beard look more real.

V-tools and u-gouges are the best tools to use for detailing beards. Start with several evenly spaced, deep strokes. Then fill the spaces in between the large cuts with smaller strokes from a smaller tool. Be sure to alternate the depth and the angles of these cuts to make the hair look more realistic. You make even want to cross the strokes over each other once in a while.

These same techniques can be used for eyebrows, mustaches and hair, too.

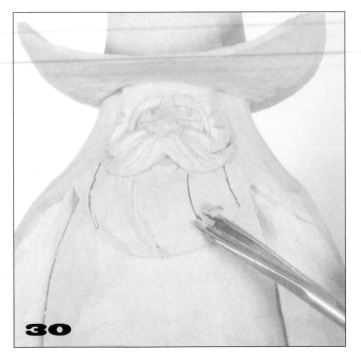

30

Start detailing the beard by making four evenly spaced grooves with a $^{1}/_{4}$" v-tool from the base of the beard to the bottom of the mustache. At the bottom of each of these grooves make a notch cut with your v-tool toward the body giving the beard a more natural appearance.

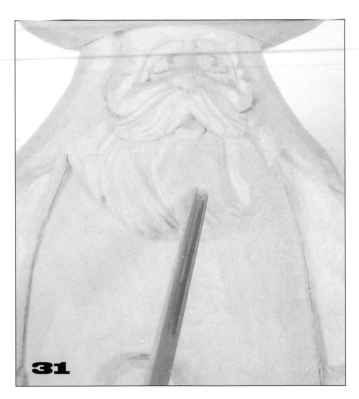

31

Using a $^{1}/_{16}$" or 2mm u-gouge, detail the beard with an upward flowing motion toward the mustache. Do not use straight cuts! Alternate the depths of the cuts and the angles of flow throughout each section of beard.

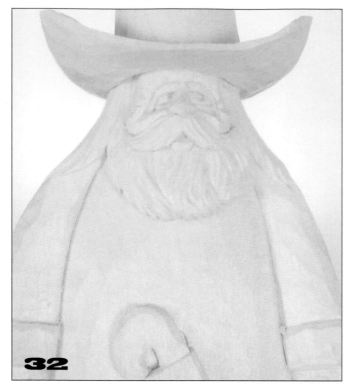

32

Congratulations! You have successfully completed a face. You will notice the following pictures do not have the completed face on them. I thought it was important that once I started directing you on the face we should complete it before going on to finish the carving.

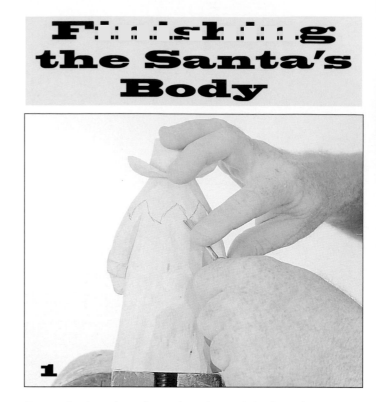

1

Draw the hair line from the edges of the beard around the back of the Santa as shown. Using a 1/4" v-tool follow the line to bring out the hair.

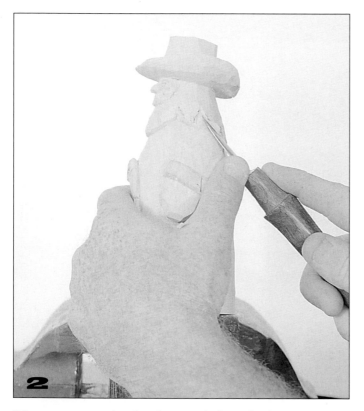

2

Using a carving knife, clean up below the hair, removing a layer of wood as shown.

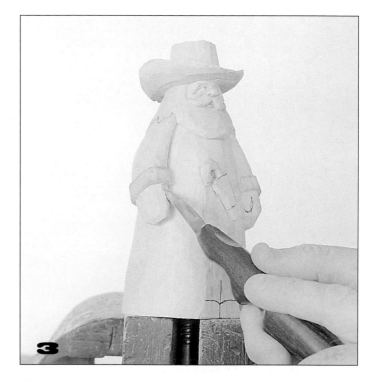

3

Draw a thumb onto the mittens as shown. Using a carving knife, make a saw cut following the lines. Cut a portion of the mitten away around the thumb to bring out the thumb and to bring the mitten away from the body.

Using the pattern, draw Santa's suit onto the front of the carving. Make sure the top of the belt is even with the top of the cuffs and the holster.

Using a carving knife, make a saw cut along the line for the coat on both sides. Once you are below the belt, make the saw cuts very deep.

Make a stop cut under the beard with a carving knife.

Then make a v-cut using a 1/4" v-tool along the coat line to the beard.

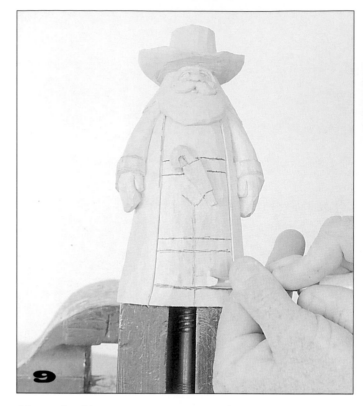

Between the belt and the beard, use your carving knife to round the body to the coat line so that the coat is 1/16" thick.

Using the 1/4" u-gouge, cut across the grain over the toe of the boot to the stop cut at the edge of the coat. This cut should be 1/4" deep at this time. The total depth will be achieved over several stages.

With a #7 fishtail gouge, cut across the grain from the bottom of the holster to the toe of the boot. This cut should be equal to the depth of the cut made in the previous step. Repeat these cuts until the desired depth is obtained. The coat edge should stick out 1/2" beyond the legs.

With a carving knife, make a 45-degree angle stop cut behind the holster and base of the candy cane. Round the holster and candy cane.

With the carving knife, saw cut across the top and bottom of belt. Then, starting 1/16" above the belt, make an angling cut down to the stop cut. Below the belt, remove wood up to the stop cut at the belt so that the belt is 1/16" thick.

Re-draw the boot cuffs and the line between the legs. The cuffs should be 1/2" deeper than outer edge of the coat when finished. With a 1/4" u-gouge cut across the grain from the bottom of the cuff to the top of the toe. This cut should be 1/8" to 1/4" deep. It will take several cuts to accomplish this depth. Once the desired depth is achieved, define the bottom of the cuff using a 1/4" v-tool.

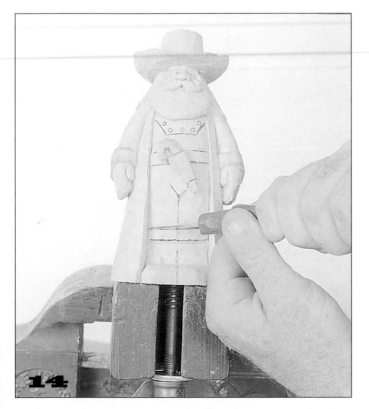

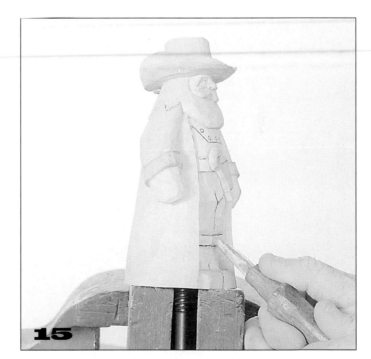

Make a saw cut across top of cuff with a carving knife. Then, make an angling cut down to the stop cut, starting 1/16" above the cuff.

Make a saw cut from the crotch to the bottom of the carving along the line between the legs. Using a carving knife, make a v-cut along the length of the legs and along crotch lines. The cut should be wider at the toe of the boots separating the boot tips 3/8". Refer to photo 18 to see the end result of this cut.

33

Push a ⅛" u-gouge into the carving to make buttons on the shirt. Raise the back end of the tool slightly to prevent the buttons from popping out. You will have to make two stab cuts for each button to create a round button.

Carefully trim any excess wood from around the buttons with a carving knife. Take care not to cut off the buttons. Continue trimming until the buttons are raised slightly above the shirt.

Make a saw cut along the button flap of the shirt with a carving knife.

Use the carving knife to trim up to the stop cut, removing a thin layer of wood between the belt and the button flap. The flap should be ¹/32" thick.

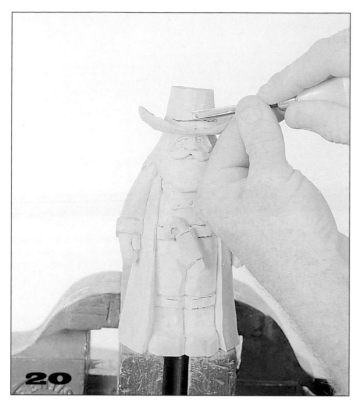

Draw on the hat band. The top of the band should be 1/4" above the top of the brim of the hat. Using a 1/4" v-tool define the hat band by cutting above the band line, recessing the hat riser 1/16".

Use a 1/4"v-tool to define where the band meets the brim of the hat.

Make a stop cut under the brim of the hat along the hair. Detail the hair with flowing upward cuts, similar to those used for the beard.

Clean up the base of the hat with your carving knife. Make sure the cuts detailing the hair are not straight. Flowing cuts will make more realistic-looking hair.

DETAILING FUR

The fur trim on this Santa's coat is smooth, but making some extra fur-like texturing on the fur cuffs and trim will add a nice touch to any Santa.

You can add details for fur with any number of tools, including a v-tool, a 2mm veiner, or a Dremel tool with a special bit. Lately, I have been experimenting with a Dremel tool outfitted with a small rough pointed bit. Stab the bit tip into the trim area about 1/16" deep over every bit of the trim's surface. The resulting cuts will give the wood a fur-like or even wool-like texture.

Viewed from the side, the Santa will look like this.

Draw on the duster flap as shown. Make a saw cut along this line. Cut up to the stop cut so that the duster flap is 1/16" thick.

To make the duster appear more flowing you should make several deep cuts from the base of the carving to the duster flap and mittens with a 1/2" u-gouge.

27

With a 1/2" u-gouge make some shallow diagonal cuts between the deep cuts. This will give the duster a flowing appearance .

28

Clean the corners of these cuts, rounding them with your carving knife.

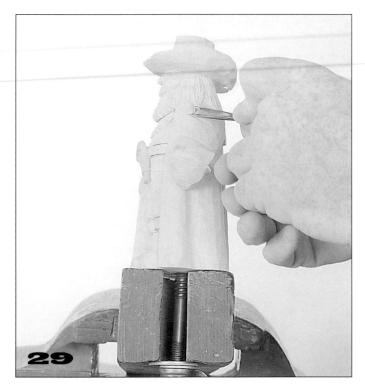

29

From the elbow to the hair line on sleeves, use a 1/4" u-gouge to make a few cuts. Again clean these up with your carving knife. This should give your Santa's duster a cloth like appearance.

30

You are now done carving your Santa! At this point sanding is optional. The more you sand, the softer the cloth appears.

Chapter Three

Painting Step-by-Step

You have two choices to finish your carved Santa—give him a painted finish or a natural finish. Either will make a beautiful finished project. The choice is dependent on your preferences.

A Natural Finish

This approach works well for carvers who try to avoid painting at all costs and for those who prefer the beauty of the wood to show through. If you choose to give your Santa a natural finish, douse the carving with a coat of linseed oil. Allow this to dry. Dab on more oil with a brush if necessary. Rub off excess. Allow the carving to dry completely. Seal with one coat of Deft semi-gloss spray.

Painting Your Santa

If you choose to paint your Santa, take some time to develop a painting schedule for your piece. If you're having trouble visualizing the colors on your Santa, try coloring in the pattern with the colors you've chosen. This will not only help you to see how the colors work with each other, but also allow you to change your mind about the colors you've chosen before you start to paint.

In the following painting demonstration, I've used acrylic paints to paint my Santa. I applied two coats of paint and used blush from a make-up kit to color the Santa's cheeks. I've used the following colors. Use these on your Santa as well, or choose colors of your own.

antique white—beard, mustache, eyebrows
white—fur trim, candy cane, buttons
barn red—hat, trim, coat
black—belt, holster, boots
gray—pants, shirt
forest green—mittens
bright red—candy cane

After the paint is dry, seal the carving with a coat of Deft semi-gloss.

Signing Your Finished Santa

Always sign and date your carving. For beginning carvers this is especially important. Years from now you will look at that first carving (I think everyone should keep that first one) and be able to see how far you have progressed. By signing and dating the piece, you will know how long ago you finished that first carving. I sign mine on the bottom of the carving, but you may choose to sign yours any where. Some carvers choose inconspicuous places, such as the back of a boot; others choose more obvious sites.

You may wish to leave your Santa with a natural finish.

If you will be painting your Santa, start by applying a cosmetic powder blush to the cheeks with a brush.

With a "0" round brush, apply antique white acrylic paint to the Santa's beard, mustache and eyebrows.

Still using a "0" round brush apply a coat of acrylic white paint to the fur trim of coat and hatband. Paint the candy cane white. Paint the buttons white.

5

With the same brush, using acrylic paint in barn red, apply paint to the hat, the trim and the coat next to the body.

7

With a larger brush paint all of the hat and the coat with the same barn red acrylic paint.

6

Continuing to use the same brush, paint the belt, the holster and the boots with black acrylic paint.

8

Santa's pants and shirt are both painted with a gray acrylic paint and a "0" round brush.

Santa Carving

Use the "0" round brush to paint the mittens with a forest green acrylic paint.

Paint the stripes on the candy cane with a very small pointed brush and a bright red acrylic paint.

Viewed from the front, the painted Santa looks like this. To finish your carving, spray it with two coats of semi-gloss Deft.

From the back, the Santa looks like this.

Chapter Four

Patterns
for Eleven
Original Santas

Bronco Bill Claus

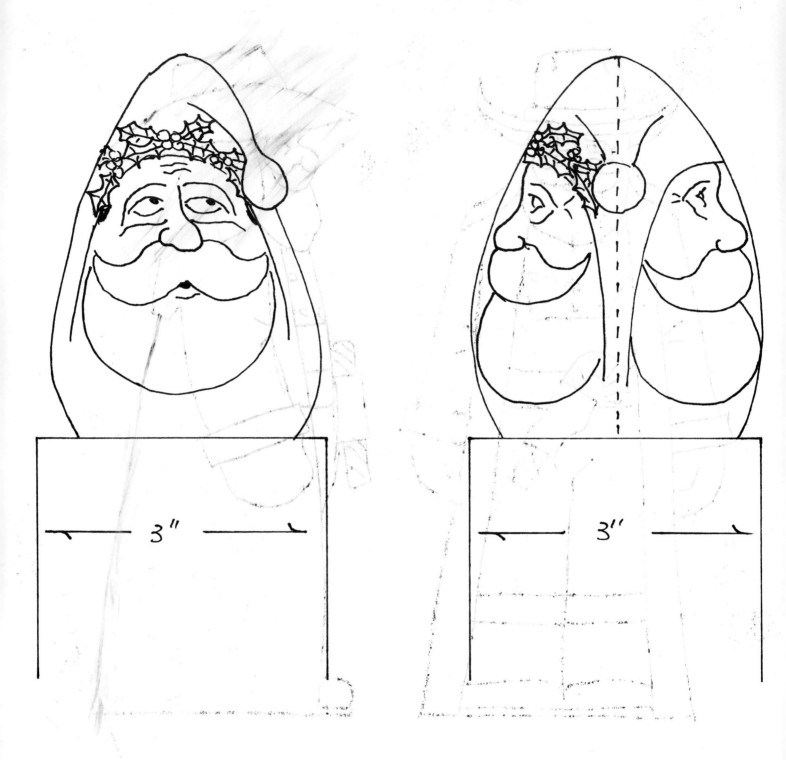

Robed Santa

Tired Santa

"Wild Bill" Santa Claus

Small Teardrop Santa (Traditional)

Small Teardrop Santa (Old World)

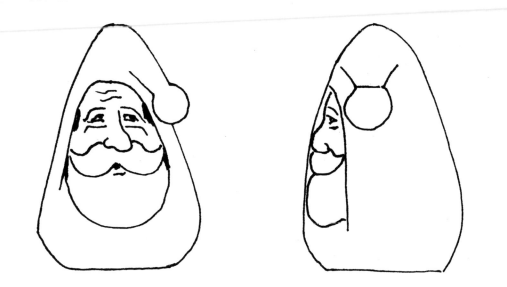

Roberts Santa

Backwoods Santa

Naughty
or Nice Santa

You are invited to Join the

National Wood Carvers Association
"Some carve their careers: others just chisel"
since 1953

If you have any interest in woodcarving: If you carve wood, create wood sculpture or even just whittle in your spare time, you will enjoy your membership in the National Wood Carvers Association. The non-profit NWCA is the world's largest carving club with over 33,000 members. There are NWCA members in more than 56 countries around the globe.

The Association's goals are to:
- promote wood carving
- foster fellowship among member enthusiasts
- encourage exhibitions and area get togethers
- list sources of equipment and information for the wood carving artist
- provide a forum for carving artists

The NWCA serves as a valuable network of tips, hints and helpful information for the wood carver. Membership is only $11.00 per year.

Members receive the magazine "Chip Chats" six times a year, free with their membership. "Chip Chats" contains articles, news events, demonstrations of technique, patterns and a full color section showcasing examples of fine craftsmanship. Through this magazine you will be kept up to date on shows and workshops to attend, new products, special offers to NWCA members and other members' activities in your area and around the world.

National Wood Carvers Association
7424 Miami Ave.
Cincinnati, OH 45243

Name: _____

Address: _____

_____

Dues $11.00 per year in USA, $14.00 per year foreign (payable in US Funds)

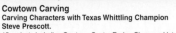